CLEAN JOKES &
HARMLESS HUMOR

1

Hamming it Up
with Rib-Tickling Humor

BY STEPHEN RATAY

Clean Jokes & Harmless Humor, Volume 1:
Hamming It Up with Rib-Tickling Humor

ISBN: 978-1-960989-01-7
LCCN: 2023936836

Published by 4L Books, Lexington, SC.

Live. Love. Learn. Laugh.

4L Books is a Christian publisher for all people. We publish remarkable new works and give new life to forgotten classics. Visit 4LBooks.com for details.

DEDICATION

Who dedicates a joke book? Me—Stephen Ratay. That's who.

It's not because I think this book is a literary masterpiece, which will endure for ages hence. It's because a sense of humor is a gift, like life itself. So I want to thank the Giver.

God carefully fashioned you a certain way. (You know that, right?) In like manner, He planted humor in my heart. Over time, it grew and was cultivated by my family.

I enjoy laughing at the simplest of things. This ability to laugh, at myself and others, has been a great asset. It soothes wounds. It softens my countenance when life is hard. It lightens my heart when circumstances are heavy.

Thank You, Jesus, for creating me, for saving me, for filling my days with laughter, and for giving me peace and enduring joy, even when life isn't so funny.

⚠ **WARNING**

This side up. Lift flap to open. Employees must wash hands before returning to work. Keep off the grass. Please don't feed the animals. Use other door. Any ideas expressed within these pages do not constitute actual legal, medical, or other professional advice. Press F1 to continue.

TABLE OF CONTENTS

FOREWARD

They laughed when I told them I wanted to write a joke book. Well, nobody's laughing now!

Since you're reading this, I'll assume you appreciate good humor, like me. A play on words. Some irony. A bit of borderline absurdity. There are lots of suitable things at which to laugh, but many "jokes" cross a boundary of good taste.

Then it's not so funny anymore.

I like to laugh, but I love my Lord. No kidding. So the best way to honor Him, while enjoying His gift of laughter, is to keep it clean. Then we all can have fun with clear consciences.

Bottom line: we published these volumes in the *Clean Jokes & Harmless Humor* series for everyone who likes to laugh.

This includes both genders and all ages, sizes, colors and backgrounds. In my most careful estimation, there's no rude or offensive content. It's just classic jokes for amateur comedians and lighthearted audiences everywhere.

INTRODUCTION

The *Clean Jokes & Harmless Humor* series is, collectively, the quintessential joke book. The volumes in this series contain most popular kinds of jokes. Each book picks up where the previous book ends.

Volume 1 begins your tour of classic comedy. Get ready for criss-crosses, funny names, knock-knocks, cafés (no bars here), and lightbulb jokes. They amuse kids and adults alike.

(These jokes have not been tested on judges, IRS agents, or any airport Customs officials. That's considered off-label use. So we cannot guarantee desired results with all demographics.)

This book could be three times as long. You don't want a bunch of filler material, though. So it's slimmed down and carefully crafted to churn out chuckles and generate guffaws.

What's that? You thought Christians were all frowns and furrowed brows? Well, if you never met a funny Christian, you've come to the right place. Just wait here; I'll go find one...

CHAPTER 1

CRISS-CROSSES

1. What do you get if you cross a chemistry set and sandpaper?
    Science friction.

2. What do you get if you cross a dinosaur and a termite?
    Dino-mite.

3. What do you get if you cross a cantaloupe and a sad dog?
    Melon collie.

4. What do you get if you cross pasta and a boa constrictor?
    Noodles that twirl themselves around your fork.

5.   What do you get if you cross a water
     balloon and a needle?
     Wet.

6.   What do you get if you cross a
     hummingbird and a doorbell?
     A humdinger.

7.   What do you get if you cross a dog and a
     calculator?
     A friend you can count on.

8.   What do you get if you cross a baseball
     player and a frog?
     *An outfielder who catches flies... and eats
     them.*

9. What do you get if you cross a rhino and an elephant?
It's not rhelephant.

10. What do you get if you cross a duck and a huge reptile?
A quack-odile.

11. What do you get if you cross a wolf and a rooster?
An animal that howls when the sun rises.

12. What do you get if you cross a goose and a bull?
An animal that honks before it runs you down.

13. What do you get if you cross a Yeti and a sloth?
The Abominably Slow Man.

14. What do you get if you cross a hawk and a finch?
    A swallow.

15. What do you get if you cross peas and carrots?
    Parrots.

16. What do you get if you cross a sea monster and a duck?
    The quacken.

17. What do you get if you cross a turtle and a porcupine?
    A slowpoke.

18. What do you get if you cross a dinosaur and a pig?
Jurassic Pork.

19. What do you get if you cross a firecracker and a lemon pie?
A boom-meringue.

20. What do you get if you cross a herding dog and a daisy?
A collie flower.

21. What do you get if you cross a sheep, a hummingbird, and a ladybug?
Bah, hum-bug.

22. What do you get if you cross an owl and a
    female goat?
    A hootenanny.

23. What do you get if you cross a sidewalk
    and a street?
    You get to the other side of the street.

24. What do you get if you cross a parrot and
    a grizzly bear?
    *I'm not sure, but when it speaks, you better
    listen.*

25. What do you get if you cross a parrot and
    a pig?
    A bird that hogs the conversation.

26. What do you get if you cross a skunk and a boomerang?
     A smell that always comes back.

27. What do you get if you cross a laboratory and an ice cream parlor?
Micro scoops.

28. What do you get if you cross a soda and a marsupial?
Coca-koala.

29. What do you get if you cross a primate and a flower?
A chimp-pansy.

30. What do you get if you cross a wolverine and a cow?
I don't know, but you better not try to milk it.

31. What do you get if you cross 50 female pigs and 50 male deer?
One hundred sows and bucks.

32. What do you get if you cross a zebra and a sheep?
A striped sweater.

33. What do you get if you cross a carrier pigeon and a woodpecker?
A bird that relays messages in Morse code.

34. What do you get if you cross a cartoon bear and a skunk?
Winnie the Phew.

35. What do you get if you cross an elephant and a kangaroo?
    Giant holes all over Australia.

36. What do you get if you cross a bat and a man?
    A ban—a lifetime ban from all genetics labs and revocation of research funding.

37. What do you get if you cross a psychiatrist and a banana peel?
    A Freudian slip.

38. What do you get if you cross a rooster and a giraffe?
    An animal that wakes up everybody on the top floor.

39. What do you get if you cross a dog and a dinosaur?
No mail, ever!

40. What do you get if you cross a snake and an engineer?
    A boa constructor.

41. What do you get if you cross a turkey and an ostrich?
    A Thanksgiving bird that buries its head in the mashed potatoes.

42. What do you get if you cow and a duck?
    Cheese and quackers.

43. What do you get if you cross a joke and a rhetorical question?

CHAPTER 2

FUNNY NAMES

44. Name a guy with short hair.
Buzz.

45. Name a baseball power-hitter.
Homer.

46. Name a male road worker.
Lane.

47. Name a lady who runs through the woods.
Brooke.

48. Name a guy whom people stare at and talk about.
Art.

49. Name a guy who overrules Congress.
     Vito.

50. Name a lady who copies people's drawings.
     Tracy.

51. Name a guy who lays by your door.
     Matt.

52. Name a retired miner.
     Doug.

53. Name a lady who stands in the middle of a
     tennis court.
     Annette.

54. Name a guy who hides under your couch.
Dusty.

55. Name a male archer.
Beau.

56. Name a male landscaper.
Moe.

57. Name a male long-distance runner.
Miles.

58. Name two ladies who live at the beach.
Sandy and Shelley.

59. Name an average guy.
    Norm.

60. Name a lady who likes bowling?
    Allie.

61. Name a guy whom you have to pay.
    Bill.

62. Name a guy who can't pay his bills.
    Owen.

63. Name a lady with only one shoe.
    Eileen.

64. Name a little girl with a wiggly tooth.
    Lucy.

65. Name a guy who speaks loudly.
Mike.

66. Name a lady who listens to loud music.
Blair.

67. Name a guy who goes with a suit.
Ty.

68. Name a guy who cut himself while shaving.
Nick.

69. Name a lady with freckles.
Dottie.

70. Name a guy who can lift a car.
Jack.

71. Name a man with an angry cat.
Claude.

72. Name a male librarian.
Reid.

73. Name a lady who sings in your tree.
Robin.

74. Name a lady who bugs people.
Nat.

75. Name a lady who complains a lot.
     Mona.

76. Name a female marksman.
Amy.

77. Name a lady who listens to Christmas music.
Carol.

78. Name a guy who sings in your tree.
Jay.

79. Name a lady who enjoys reading.
Paige.

80. Name a guy who lives underground.
Cole.

81. Name a male meteorologist.
     Sonny.

82. Name a female meteorologist.
     Haley.

83. Name a guy who says what he means.
     Frank.

84. Name a guy who means what he says.
     Earnest.

85. Name a female magician.
     Trixie.

86. Name a pastor who drives too fast.
   Rev.

87. Name a butcher.
   Chuck.

88. Name his daughter.
   Patty.

89. And how does he introduce her?
   "Meet Patty."

90. Name a male weightlifter.
   Jim.

91. Name a guy with a magnifying glass.
Seymour.

92. Name a guy who collects old jars.
     Mason.

93. Name a male florist.
     Bud.

94. Name a lady who likes to gamble.
     Bette.

95. Name a male computer programmer.
     Codi.

96. Name a male DNA researcher.
     Gene.

97. Name a girl who likes basic math?
Addy.

98. Name a pale-faced lady.
Blanche.

99. Name a male mountain climber.
Cliff.

100. Name a lady who wakes up early.
Dawn.

101. Name a guy who prays on his knees.
Neil.

102. Name a guy who works in the hospital.
Ward.

103. Name a female lawyer.
Sue.

104. Name a magician who lost his magic.
Ian.

105. Name a Frenchman in sandals.
Philippe Phloppe.

106. Lance isn't a common name nowadays, but in medieval times, men were named Lance a lot.

CHAPTER 3

KNOCK-KNOCKS

107. Knock, knock.
Who's there?
Hutch.
Hutch, who?
Bless you!

108. Knock, knock.
Who's there?
Nana.
Nana, who?
Nana your business.

109. Knock, knock.
Who's there?
Barbie.
Barbie, who?
Barbie Q.

110. Knock, knock.
     Who's there?
     Toby.
     Toby, who?
     Toby, or not Toby? That is the question.

111. Knock, knock.
     Who's there?
     Tank.
     Tank, who?
     You're welcome.

112. Knock, knock.
     Who's there?
     Oswald.
     Oswald, who?
     Oswald my gum!

113. Knock, knock.
Who's there?
Cook.
Cook, who?
Hey! Who are you calling cuckoo?

114. Knock, knock.
Who's there?
Interrupting Raven.
Inter...
CAAAWWWW!

115. Knock, knock.
Who's there?
Althea.
Althea, who?
Althea later alligator.

116. Knock, knock.
Who's there?
Kanga.
Kanga, who?
Kangaroo.

117. Knock, knock.
     Who's there?
     Icing.
     Icing, who?
     Icing because I'm happy!

118. Knock, knock.
     Who's there.
     Mike.
     Mike, who?
     Mike Robe. I'm very small.

119. Knock, knock.
     Who's there?
     Zeke.
     Zeke, who?
     Zeke and you shall find.

120. Knock, knock.
     Who's there?
     Boo.
     Boo, who?
     Don't cry. It's just a joke.

121. Knock, knock.
     Who's there?
     Annie.
     Annie, who?
     Annie-body home?

122. Knock, knock.
     Who's there?
     Otto.
     Otto, who?
     Otto know why you won't open the door.

123. Knock, knock.
     Who's there?
     Razor.
     Razor, who?
     Razor hand if you have a question.

124. Knock, knock.
     Who's there?
     Francis.
     Francis, who?
     Francis next to Spain.

125. Knock, knock.
     Who's there?
     Two-Knee.
     Two-Knee, who?
     Two-Knee fish sandwich.

126. Knock, knock.
Who's there?
Sombrero.
Sombrero, who?
Sombrero-ver the rainbow... (singing)

127. Knock, knock.
Who's there?
Ice Cream Soda.
Ice Cream Soda, who?
Ice Cream Soda people can hear me.

128. Knock, knock.
Who's there?
Yeah.
Yeah, who?
Giddyup cowboy (or cowgirl)!

129. Knock, knock.
Who's there?
Halibut.
Halibut, who?
Halibut you let me inside?

130. Knock, knock.
    Who's there?
    Irish.
    Irish, who?
    Irish I could cheer you up.

131. Knock, knock.
    Who's there?
    Nuisance.
    Nuisance, who?
    What's nuisance yesterday?

132. Knock, knock.
    Who's there?
    Auntie.
    Auntie, who?
    Auntie Disestablishmentarianism.

133. Knock, knock.
Who's there?
Amish.
Amish, who?
Amish the good old days.

134. Knock, knock.
Who's there?
Yoda Lady.
Yoda Lady, who?
I didn't know you can yodel.

135. Knock, knock.
Who's there?
Alma.
Alma, who?
Alma friends have forgotten me.

136. Knock, knock.
     Who's there?
     Police.
     Police, who?
     Police to meet you.

137. Knock, knock.
    Who's there?
    Repeat.
    Repeat, who?
    Okay. Who. Who. Who...

138. Knock, knock.
    Who's there?
    Amarillo.
    Amarillo, who?
    Amarillo fashioned guy (or gal).

139. Knock, knock.
    Who's there?
    Orange.
    Orange, who?
    Orange you glad to see me?

140. Knock, knock.
Who's there?
Jamaican.
Jamaican, who?
Jamaican me crazy.

141. Knock, knock.
Who's there?
Mary.
Mary, who?
Mary Christmas!

142. Knock, knock.
Who's there?
Abbey.
Abbey, who?
Abbey New Year! (Abbey Birthday!)

143. Knock, knock.
Who's there?
Eyesore.
Eyesore, who?
Eyesore do love you.

144. Knock, knock.
Who's there?
Spell.
Spell, who?
Okay. W-h-o.

145. Knock, knock.
Who's there?
Shelby.
Shelby, who?
Shelby coming round the mountain when she comes... (singing)

146. Knock, knock.
Who's there?
Donut.
Donut, who?
Donut open the door to strangers!

147. Knock, knock.
Who's there?
Hike.
Hike, who?
I didn't know you like Japanese poetry.

148. Knock, knock.
Who's there?
Dishes.
Dishes, who?
Dishes me. Who are you?

149. Knock, knock.
Who's there?
Control Freak. Now you say, "Control Freak, who?"

CHAPTER 4

AT THE CAFÉ

150. A man walks into a library and asks for a cheeseburger and fries.

     "Sir, this is a library," answers the librarian.

     "Sorry," he whispers. "Can I have it now?"

151. **Woman:** Waiter, this egg is bad.

     Waiter: It's not my fault. I only laid the table.

152. **Waiter:** I'm really sorry about your wait.

     Customer: Are you saying I'm fat?

153. **Man:** Please bring me a cup of coffee, with no cream.

     Waiter: I'm sorry, but we're out of cream. How about with no milk?

154. A man walks into a café with a set of jumper cables, and asks for a soda.
"Okay," says the waitress. "But don't start anything."

155. **Woman:** This soup tastes funny.
Waiter: Then why aren't you laughing?

156. **Man:** Waiter, there's a worm on my plate!
Waitress: That's your sausage, sir.

157. A dog walks into a café and orders a coffee.
Waitress: Wow, a talking dog! You should work at the circus.
Dog: The circus is hiring web developers?

158. **Woman:** Excuse me. What's in the "Liar Sandwich"?
Waitress: Oh, that's full of baloney.

159. A clickbait marketer walks into a café. You'll be AMAZED by the SURPRISING thing that happens next...

160. **Man:** This coffee tastes like dirt!
Waiter: It was ground this morning.

161. Two peanuts were sitting peacefully in a café, but one was a salted.

162. **Woman:** Waiter, your thumb is in my soup!
Waiter: Don't worry, ma'am. It's not hot at all.

163. **Man 1:** Look, this place serves cow tongue.
Man 2: Gross! I won't eat anything that came out of an animal's mouth. I'll just order eggs.

164. **Man:** Waiter, there's a dead fly in my soup!
Waiter: It's because the heat always kills them.

165. **Man:** Do you have any specials?
Waiter: No, sir. There's nothing special about the food here.

166. A restaurant is the only place where people are happy when they're fed up.

167. A man walks into a café with a small lizard on his shoulder.
Host: What do you call that thing?
Man: I named him Tiny; he's my newt.

168. **Man:** Waiter, will my pizza be long?
Waiter: No sir. It will be round.

169. **Man:** Waitress, there's a fly in my butter!
Waitress: That's not a fly, sir; it's a roach.
And its not butter either; it's margarine.

170. A potato walks into a café. All eyes are on
him.

171. **Man:** Waiter, I'd like a steak.
Waiter: What do you want with it?
Man: If it's the same as last time, a hammer
and chisel.

172. **Woman:** Waiter, there's a fly in my stew!
     Waiter: The rotten meat attracts them.

173. **Man:** Waiter, what's this fly doing in my soup?
     Waiter: He's praying, sir.
     Man: I can't eat this. Take it away.
     Waiter: See? His prayers were answered.

174. Two conspiracy theorists, who don't know each other, walk into a café at the same time. There's no way that was just a coincidence.

175. **Man:** Why is your thumb on my steak?
     Waitress: Sorry. I just didn't want it to fall on the floor again.

176. **Man:** This food isn't fit for a pig!

 Waiter: Sorry. I'll bring you some that is.

177. **Woman:** What's this fly doing in my soup?
Waiter: Drowning, ma'am.

178. **Woman:** Waiter, what's this in my soup?
Waitress: I'm not entirely sure. I can't tell one bug from another.

179. A penguin waddles into a café and asks the host, "Did my brother come in here?" The host replies, "I don't know. What does he look like?"

180. A mushroom walks into a café.
Hostess: No mushrooms allowed.
Mushroom: Why not? I'm a fun guy.

181. **Woman:** You forgot to bring my honey.
     Waiter: Where should I look for him?

182. **Woman:** Waiter, there's a fly in my soup!
     Waiter: Sorry. I thought I had removed all of them.

183. **Woman:** Waiter, there's no chicken in this chicken soup!
     Waiter: Right. Well, you won't find any horses in the horseradish either.

184. A cow walks into a café.
     Host: Hey!
     Cow: You read my mind.

185. Then the hostess says, "We don't serve time travelers in here."
A time traveler walks into a café.

186. As a tapeworm slithers into a café, a waitress screams, "Get out, you hideous parasite!"
The tapeworm remarks smugly, "You're a lousy host."

187. **Waiter:** What would you two like to drink?
Man 1: I'll have a soda.
Man 2: Me too, in a clean glass.
Waiter (after returning): Here you go—two sodas. Who asked for the clean glass?

188. **Woman:** How long will my sub sandwich be?
Waiter: Ten inches.

189. A bear ambles into a café and growls, "I'd like a steak... and a soda."
The waiter asks, "Why the big pause?"

190. A baseball player runs into a café, and the owner throws him out.

191. **Man:** Is there pasta on the menu today?
Waiter: No, sir. I cleaned it off.

192. **Waiter:** Do you wanna box for your leftovers?
Customer: No, but I'll wrestle you for them.

193. A horse trots into a café, and the host asks, "Hey buddy, why the long face?"

194. **Woman:** Do you serve crabs here?
Waiter: Yes, ma'am. We serve anybody.

195. Where do young cows eat lunch?
     At the calf-eteria.

196. **Woman:** Waiter, there's a hair in my soup!
     Waiter: Of course, ma'am. It's rabbit stew.

197. A cat walks into a café, then out, then back in, and then out again...

198. A magician walked down the street and then turned into a café.

199. **Man:** Waitress, bring me some alligator soup, and make it snappy.

200. A Roman walks into a café, holds up two fingers, and orders, "I'll take five sandwiches to go, please."

201. A weasel walks into a café, and the waiter asks the weasel if he'd like something to drink. "Pop", goes the weasel.

202. A pregnant woman sits down in a café and is soon approached by a man.
Man: Do you mind if I sit here with you?
Woman: Sorry. I'm expecting somebody.

203. **Woman:** Please bring me a burnt steak, cold potatoes, and a wilted salad.
Waiter: We don't have food like that, ma'am.
Woman: That's what you served me last time.

CHAPTER 5

LIGHTBULBS

204. How many therapists does it take to change a lightbulb?
One, but only if the lightbulb truly wants to change.

205. How many real men does it take to change a lightbulb?
None. Real men aren't afraid of the dark.

206. How many real estate agents does it take to change a lightbulb ?
Ten, but we'll accept nine.

207. How many country music singers does it take to change a lightbulb?
Four. One to handle the bulb, and three to sing about how they'll miss the old one.

208. How many mystery writers does it take to change a lightbulb?
Two. One screws it most of the way, and the other gives it a surprising twist at the end.

209. How many jugglers does it take to change a lightbulb?
One, but he needs three bulbs.

210. How many stockbrokers does it take to change a lightbulb?
Sell it now, before it crashes!

211. How many telemarketers does it take to change a lightbulb?
One, but she'll only do it while you're eating dinner.

212. How many New Yorkers does it take to change a lightbulb?
Fuggedaboutit.

213. How many chiropractors does it take to change a lightbulb?
One, but it requires at least four visits.

214. How many Jewish mothers does it take to change a lightbulb?
Don't worry about me. I'll just sit here in the dark.

215. How many narcissists does it take to change a lightbulb?
One. He just holds the lightbulb while the world revolves around him.

216. How many carpenters does it take to change a lightbulb?
Two. One to hold it, and one to hammer it in.

217. How many aerospace engineers does it take to change a lightbulb?
None. It doesn't take a rocket scientist.

218. How many emergency room personnel does it take to change a lightbulb?
Four. One receptionist, two nurses, and a doctor, but it will be a three-hour wait.

219. How many South Americans does it take to change a lightbulb?
A Brazilian.

220. How many beta testers does it take to change a lightbulb?
None. They just find the problems; they don't fix them.

221. How many hippies does it take to change a lightbulb?
One, but the lava lamp has to cool off first.

222. How many high school students does it take to change a lightbulb?
An entire Facebook group, and they'll livestream the event.

223. How many optometrists does it take to change a lightbulb?
One, or two? One, or two?

224. How many firemen does it take to change a lightbulb?
Four, one to change the bulb and three to cut a hole in the roof.

225. How many magicians does it take to change a lightbulb?
That depends on what you want to change it into.

226. How many drummers it take to change a lightbulb?
One. Two. A one—two—three—four...

227. How many health nuts does it take to change a lightbulb?
First, let's look at the ingredients.

228. How many NASCAR drivers does it take to change a lightbulb?
None, they can only turn left.

229. How many roaches does it take to change a lightbulb?
     Nobody knows. When the light turns on, they scatter.

230. How many librarians does it take to change a lightbulb?
I'm not sure, but I can look that up for you.

231. How many tropical birds does it take to change a lightbulb?
Toucan do it.

232. How many CIA agents does it take to change a lightbulb?
One to <deleted> and another to <deleted> while <deleted> with a <deleted>.

233. How many Mexicans does it take to change a lightbulb?
Only Juan.

234. How many movie directors does it take to change a lightbulb?
One, but he wants to redo it until it's perfect.

235. How many police detectives does it take to change a lightbulb?
None. It turned itself in.

236. How many HOA members does it take to change a lightbulb?
At least five, and it must look the same as every other lightbulb in the neighborhood.

237. How many marketing agencies does it take to change a lightbulb?
Let's replace that old bulb with a neon light.

238. How many pessimists does it take to change a lightbulb?
It doesn't matter. The new one probably won't work anyway.

239. How many webmasters does it take to change a lightbulb?
404 (Not found).

240. How many Germans does it take to change a lightbulb?
One. They're efficient and unfunny.

241. How did the hipster burn his hand?
He changed the lightbulb before it was cool.

242. How many tourists does it take to change a lightbulb?
Three. One to hold the map, and two to ask random passers-by for directions.

243. How many bodybuilders does it take to change a lightbulb?

    Two. One to change it, straining in front of a mirror, while a spotter stands next to him and says, "You can do it, bro."

244. How many bureaucrats does it take to change a lightbulb?

    Three. There's a lot of paperwork involved, and it will cost you $50 for the permit.

245. How many fishermen does it take to change a lightbulb?

    One, and you should've seen the size of that lightbulb. It was this big (holding up hands)!

246. How many dentists does it take to change a lightbulb?
Three. One to inject anesthetic, one to extract the lightbulb, and one to offer the socket a small cup of pink bubble gum mouthwash.

247. How many surgeons does it take to change a lightbulb?
None. They wait for a suitable donor and perform a filament transplant.

248. How many UFO believers does it take to change a lightbulb?
One, alone, but he took a picture. See that dark, blurry shape? Squint your eyes a little.

249. How many editors does it take to change a lightbulb?
Let's re-phrase that question to, "The task of changing a lightbulb requires how many editors?

250. "How many IRS agents does it take to change a lightbulb?
More every year, and the bulb gets really screwed.

251. How many psychologists does it take to change a lightbulb?
One. How does that make you feel?

252. How many procrastinators does it take to change a lightbulb?
One, but he'll do it later.

253. How many talk show hosts does it take to change a lightbulb?
Three. One to screw in the new bulb, one to ask the old bulb how it feels to be replaced, and one to take questions from the audience.

254. How many road workers does it take to change a lightbulb?
Eight. One to change the bulb, and seven others to stand around watching him.

255. How many nuclear engineers does it take to change a lightbulb?
Six. One to install the new bulb, and five to figure out what to do with the old bulb for the next 10,000 years.

256. How many DIYers does it take to screw in a lightbulb?
One, but the job lasts two weekends and requires eight trips to the hardware store.

CONCLUSION

4L Books is a small Christian publisher. We produce books for all people. Our mission is to publish remarkable new works and give new life to forgotten classics.

We hope you've found value in this book. Please consider leaving feedback on Amazon or any site where this book is sold. Positive reviews attract other readers. In addition, I read your feedback and appreciate and consider every thoughtful word.

Visit 4LBooks.com for articles, news, and reviews. You can contact us there too, with suggestions or corrections. Check out our other books while you're there.

We appreciate you.

God bless,

Stephen Ratay

4L Books - Live. Love. Learn. Laugh.

Books in this Series

Clean Jokes & Harmless Humor, Volume 1:
Hamming It Up with Rib-Tickling Humor

Clean Jokes & Harmless Humor, Volume 2:
Short Funny Jokes for Kids, Adults & Dads

Clean Jokes & Harmless Humor, Volume 3:
Nutty Jokes & Stockpiles of Silliness

Clean Jokes & Harmless Humor, Volume 4:
Head-Scratching Riddles to Drive You Bananas

Clean Jokes & Harmless Humor, Volume 5:
Legendary One-Liners for Colorful Characters

www.ingramcontent.com/pod-product-compliance
Lightning Source LLC
Chambersburg PA
CBHW060133050426
42448CB00010B/2103